PUSHUPS and CRUNCHES

By Aaron & Amanda Rosen

Illustrated by Erica Olson

Those pushups and crunches!
Those pushups and crunches!

I do not like those pushups and crunches!

Would you like them on a box?

Would you like them on long walks?

Not on a box. Not on long walks.

Not in the house. Not with my spouse.

I would not do them here or there.

I would not do them anywhere.

I would not do pushups and crunches.

I do not like them,
my honey bunches.

Would you? Could you? At the Gym?

Do them! Do them!

You'll get trim.

I would not, could not, at the gym.

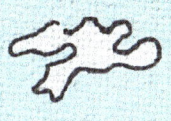
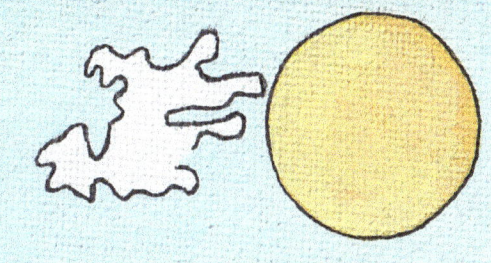

You may like them. You will see.

You may like them by the sea!

I would not, could not by the sea.

Not at the gym! You let me be.

I do not like them on a box.
I do not like them on long walks.

I do not like them in the house.
I do not like them with my spouse.

I do not like them here or there.

I do not like them anywhere.

I do not like pushups and crunches.

I do not like them, my honey bunches.

Your friends! Your friends!

Your friends! Your friends!

Could you, would you, with your friends?

Not with my friends! Not at the gym!

Not by the sea! Honey Bunches! Let me be!

I would not, could not, on a box.
I could not, would not, on long walks.

I will not do them in the house.
I will not do them with my spouse.

I will not do them here or there.
I will not do them anywhere.

I do not do
pushups and crunches.
I do not like them,
my honey bunches.

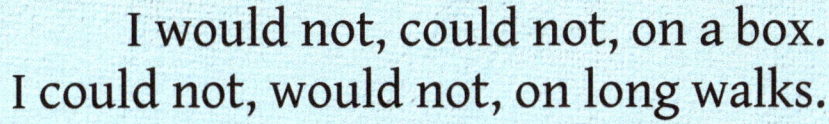

Say! At the park? Here at the park!

Would you, could you, at the park?

I would not, could not, at the park.

Would you, could you, just pretend?

I would not, could not, just pretend.
Not at the park. Not with my friends.

Not at the gym. Not by the sea.
I do not like them,
Honey Bunches, you see.

Not in the house. Not on a box.
Not with my spouse. Not on long walks.

I will not do them here or there.
I do not like them anywhere!

I do not like them,

Honey Bunches.

I could not, would not, on a log.
I will not, will not, with the dog.
I will not do them, not even pretend.
I will not do them with my friends.

Not at the park! Not by the sea!
Not at the gym! You let me be!

I do not like them on a box.
I do not like them on long walks.
I will not do them in the house.
I do not like them with my spouse.

I do not like them here or there.
I do not like them ANYWHERE!

I do not like

pushups and crunches!

I do not like them,

my honey bunches.

You do not like them.

So you say.

Try them! Try them!

And you may.

Try them and you may, I say.

Honey Bunches!

If you will let me be,

I will try them.

You will see.

Say!

I like pushups and crunches

I do! I like them,

my honey bunches!

And I would do them on a log.

And I would do them with the dog...

And I will do them, not just pretend.

And at the park. And with my friends.

And at the gym. And by the sea. They are so good, so good, you see!

So I will do them on a box.

And I will do them on long walks.

And I will do them in the house.

And I will do them with my spouse.

And I will do them here and there.

Say! I will do them ANYWHERE!

I do so like

pushups and crunches!

Thank you!

Thank you,

my honey bunches!

For our boys.

May you always choose the path of great health.

In honor of one of the greatest doctors

who wasn't a doctor at all,

but he loved all children,

no matter how big, or how small.

We give thanks to God for putting dreams in our

hearts and the ability to follow through with them.

PUSHUPS AND CRUNCHES

Copyright © 2021 by Rosen House Books

All rights reserved. No part of this book may be used or reproduced in any manner whatsoever without written permission from the publisher. Thank you for purchasing an authorized edition of this book and for complying with copyright laws by not reproducing, scanning, or distributing any part of it in any form without permission. You are supporting writers and their hard work by doing this.

LIBRARY OF CONGRESS CATALOGING-IN-PUBLICATION DATA IS AVAILABLE
ISBN 978-1-7364973-0-2

Printed in the United States of America

10 9 8 7 6 5 4 3 2 1
First Edition: April 2021

www.ingramcontent.com/pod-product-compliance
Lightning Source LLC
Chambersburg PA
CBHW040747020526
44118CB00040B/2718